Jim Thorpe

Jim Thorpe

By Thomas Fall

Illustrated by John Gretzer

Thomas Y. Crowell Company • New York

Crowell Biographies
Edited by SUSAN BARTLETT WEBER

LEONARD BERNSTEIN *by Molly Cone*

WILT CHAMBERLAIN *by Kenneth Rudeen*

CESAR CHAVEZ *by Ruth Franchere*

SAMUEL CLEMENS *by Charles Michael Daugherty*

CHARLES DREW *by Roland Bertol*

ELEANOR ROOSEVELT *by Jane Goodsell*

MARIA TALLCHIEF *by Tobi Tobias*

JIM THORPE *by Thomas Fall*

MALCOLM X *by Arnold Adoff*

Copyright © 1970 by DONALD SNOW
Illustrations copyright © 1970 by JOHN GRETZER

L.C. Card 72–94793

ISBN: 0-690-46217-4
0-690-46218-2 (LB)

5150

2   3   4   5   6   7   8   9   10

Jim Thorpe

Jim Thorpe's family were Sac and Fox Indians. They lived on a ranch in Oklahoma Territory.

Most of the Sac and Fox stayed on the Indian reservation. But Jim's father was independent and did not like reservation life. He started the ranch some twenty miles away.

The other Indians built grass huts, just as their ancestors had done. But Jim's father wanted his house to be warm and dry. Near a winding river he built a cabin out of logs for his family.

Jim's father's name was Hiram Thorpe. He was a huge man—the champion wrestler among his people. Because his first son, George, was not very athletic, Hiram had a secret wish. If we have another son, he often thought, I will teach him to wrestle at an early age. I will also teach him to run fast and to jump.

He confided his dream to his wife, Charlotte. She said, "If we have another son, Hiram, he must go to school."

Hiram wanted another son. Finally the day he was waiting for arrived. On a bright May morning in 1888 Jim Thorpe was born. And, to everyone's surprise, so was his twin brother, Charlie.

Their excited father said, "This is wonderful. Each of my new sons will have a brother exactly his own age. They will be a perfect match for wrestling and running and jumping."

2

Their mother said, "And they will keep each other company when we send them to school."

As their father predicted, the twins became well-matched competitors. Charlie would say, "Jim, I'll beat you to the river and back!"

And Jim would answer, "Nobody beats Jim!" Their father noticed that Jim always won the contests.

When the twins were old enough they were sent to the Sac and Fox reservation school. Chil-

dren from many tribes went to school there. Those who lived nearby went each day. Others who lived farther away, like Jim, boarded at the school and went home only on holidays.

From the beginning, Jim and Charlie were the best athletes in their class. Jim always came in first, and Charlie always came in second.

Their teachers believed that Charlie tried so hard to win against his brother that he exhausted himself. He became sick one winter, and the sickness turned into pneumonia. There were no hospitals in the Indian country, nor even any doctors. Jim's family did everything possible for Charlie, but he finally died. It was the first of many sad things that happened to Jim Thorpe.

Without his brother to run and jump with, Jim became a very quiet boy. When he returned to the boarding school, he could not stand it. He

4

did not care for the ball games or the running contests without Charlie.

One morning before daybreak he slipped quietly from his bed and started for home. Because he had a long way to go, he did not try to run all the way. Even at that age, Jim had a natural instinct for pacing himself.

By steady walking he arrived home around noon. His father stood in the yard at the front door of the cabin.

"I've quit school," Jim said. He watched his father's face for any sign of forgiveness. But he saw none.

"Son," Jim's father said, "have I told you why a boy must get right back on a horse that has just thrown him?"

"So the boy won't have time to think about it and get afraid," said Jim.

"That is correct. And that's why you are going back to school this very afternoon."

Hiram Thorpe then turned his son around and they began the twenty-three-mile march back to school.

"My great-grandfather Black Hawk never went to school," Jim argued.

"There were no schools when Black Hawk was a boy," his father said.

"But he became a great chief," said Jim. "Why do I need to go to school?"

"Because our old way of life is gone. We need to know about many things besides hunting and fishing. You must have an education."

"Why doesn't George have to go to school?"

"He is already too old. When he was your age, there was no school for him to go to."

Jim fell silent. But as they walked along the dusty road, he made up his mind to run away again.

At the school, he waited inside the gate until his father was out of sight. Then he ran across the yard, climbed through the fence, and darted into the scrub-oak woods.

He was not sure where he intended to go until he felt well-hidden in the woods. But once there, he knew he would not stop. He would cut through the hills and beat his father home. He would talk to his mother and try to make her see that going to school was a waste of time.

For the third time that day, the troubled boy made the trip all the way by foot. Across country, instead of on the road, the distance was only eighteen miles. And he ran every step of the way.

Jim's parents did not know what to do with

him. They felt sorry for him because they knew how much he missed his twin brother. His mother said, "If we let you stay at home this year, will you go to Haskell Institute next fall?"

Haskell was an Indian school in Kansas. Jim was frightened by the idea of going so far away, but he said eagerly, "Yes, I will."

"You'll not be able to run away from there," his father told him. "It's more than a hundred miles from here."

All that winter, spring, and summer, Jim stayed on the ranch. He hunted and rode with his older brother George. He learned to bulldog calves and help with the roundup. He learned to stalk deer along the river and bring down venison for the family table. When fall arrived, he was ready for school again.

"I won't come home this time unless you send for me," he told his father as he boarded the train for Kansas.

At Haskell Institute, Jim touched a football for the first time in his life. The star of the school team was a husky Indian named Archiquette. Jim watched him kicking the ball one day. "I never saw a ball like that," he said, "with a point on each end."

"It's called a football," said Archiquette.

"Can I hold it for a minute?" asked Jim.

The football star handed him the ball. Jim stared at it, turning it over and over. "Can I try to kick it?"

"Go ahead."

Jim stepped forward with three quick strides. He booted the football. It sailed up and away, far over the heads of the other players on the field.

Archiquette looked at the boy in amazement. "How old are you?" he asked.

"Eleven," said Jim.

"What's your name?"

"Jim Thorpe."

"When you grow up, you can be a great football player, if you want to," said Archiquette.

"I'm going to be," said Jim, more excited than he had ever been in his life.

Archiquette took the boy under his wing at Haskell. Jim followed his hero everywhere. He learned to throw, kick, and run with the ball. He was happy again at last.

And then a sad and frightening thing happened. The school received word that Jim's father had been wounded in a hunting accident.

Jim ran away from the school. If he had waited, he would have been sent home on the train. But he did not know that.

He traveled the entire distance—one hundred twenty-five miles—by foot. He ran swiftly for a while and then jogged for a while. He swam rivers and streams, stopping to rest only when exhausted. He slept in the woods and in barns along the way. He got lost a few times. He even begged at farmhouses for food. Once he hopped a freight train, only to learn that it was going in the wrong direction.

He reached home at last—almost two weeks

after leaving the institute. His father, he learned, was much better. But now his mother had become sick. Before his father recovered from the hunting wound, his mother died.

Jim never returned to Haskell. He stayed at home and helped his brother George on the ranch. Together they nursed their father back to health.

During the next few years Jim learned to catch wild horses and break them to the saddle. He earned money by selling them to other ranchers nearby. When he was fifteen, he began to think about going to school somewhere and trying to play football. He also considered going farther west to look for a job.

One day a teacher from Carlisle, Pennsylvania, came to the Sac and Fox country looking for students. Carlisle was the site of a famous Indian school. The teacher learned that Jim liked football.

14

"We have a good team at Carlisle," he urged. "Why don't you come there with me?"

Jim talked to the teacher for hours, and he decided to go. I am fifteen now, he said to himself, feeling almost grown. I can play football.

He discovered at Carlisle, however, that he was not grown yet. The football players were much older and heavier. He knew it would be a few years before he could make the team. But still he hoped the coach would notice him.

One afternoon he finally got a break.

The coach was a man named Warner. Everyone called him Pop. Sometimes, to begin practice, he would select one boy to try running the ball past all the others, just to see how far he could get.

This time Pop Warner looked at Jim. "Do you want to try it, young fellow?" he asked.

"Yes!" Jim cried, and ran to take his position. He nearly stumbled over his own feet in his excitement.

The other players scattered across the field, waiting to tackle him. If Jim was afraid, the fear left him the moment Pop threw him the ball.

That football felt wonderful in his hands. He tucked it into the crook of his arm. As the tacklers bore down on him, he pretended to be dodging through scrub oaks and leaping across streams back home. It seemed the most natural thing in the world.

Tackler after tackler tried to bring him down. But Jim swiveled and dodged. When he got into the open, he simply outran the other players to the goal line.

But Pop Warner did not praise him. Instead, the coach scolded the other players. "He isn't even old enough to make the team," Pop shouted.

"He made you look like a bunch of girls out there! Now, line up and let's try that once more."

Jim got ready to try again. The squad took its position. Jim caught the ball and ran toward the tacklers.

This time he imagined himself in the path of a herd of wild horses. They thundered toward him, and he stopped suddenly. He whirled as they hit him, and spun himself loose. He ducked his head

and darted forward. Soon he was in the clear again. And again he reached the goal line, saying to himself, Nobody catches Jim!

After practice that evening, Pop Warner called him over. "I don't know your name, son."

"Jim Thorpe," said Jim proudly.

"You run pretty well. Report for track tomorrow."

"I'd . . . rather play football, sir."

"You're not big enough. But you can make the

track team if you work hard. What tribe are you from?"

"The Sac and Fox, Oklahoma Territory."

The coach studied him thoughtfully. "You're going to play football for me someday, Jim. But while you're young, we're not taking a chance on getting you hurt. Did you ever throw a javelin?"

"No, but I have killed deer with a spear," Jim said.

"How far can you run?"

"I don't know, sir. I once ran eighteen miles—but that was as far as I had to go that day."

Pop Warner grinned. He knew that something big was in store for this boy—and for Carlisle. But Jim did not know it. He only knew that he wanted to play football now, and they would not let him.

The following year, Jim received word from

his brother George that their father had died. George was closing the ranch.

Jim felt lost. He had always planned to return to the ranch after finishing school. Now, without his father to encourage him, he wondered whether school was worthwhile. He began losing interest in his classwork.

In the spring he heard that a group of baseball players were going to play on a team in North Carolina. "Why don't you go with us, Jim?" one of them asked. "We'll be paid fifteen dollars a week. And we need a pitcher."

"Paid?" Jim asked, surprised. "For playing ball?"

Because he was so lonely, Jim left Carlisle and went with his new friends to North Carolina. That season he pitched twenty-five games and won twenty-three of them. It was clear to everyone who knew him that Jim did well at any sport he tried.

After the baseball season, he went back to the Indian country. Nobody knew where his brother was. The cabin on the river was empty. The ranch was bare except for wild horses and a few stray cattle.

He spent the winter alone. Then he got a job on a nearby ranch. He was not happy, but he was ashamed to return to Carlisle after having run

away. He worked on the ranch for another year as a broncobuster. Then one day he received a letter from Pop Warner.

"I keep thinking about you, Jim," Pop wrote. "You must be big enough to make the football team by now. Why don't you come back to school?"

Jim caught the next train to Pennsylvania.

In no time at all he was a first-string halfback. With Jim Thorpe carrying the ball, passing, and kicking, the Carlisle team won game after game. They beat Harvard, Yale, Pittsburgh, Chicago, and many other big schools.

Once Jim played against a West Point army cadet named Dwight Eisenhower. Everyone called the cadet Ike. He was the same Ike who later became a famous general and then President of the United States.

President Eisenhower often told the story of the day he played against Carlisle. The West Point coach said to him, "Ike, get in there and stop that Indian!"

Ike raced onto the field. "The next time Thorpe runs toward us," he said to a teammate, "I'll hit him high and you hit him low." In this way they would show the Indian that nobody could run over West Point.

Ike soon had his opportunity. Thorpe came toward him like a bull on the range. The great Indian and the future President met with a thundering crash. When the dust settled, cadet Eisenhower was in a heap on the ground. Thorpe had carried the ball right over him for a long gain.

Everyone in America who was interested in sports now talked about the football-playing Indian from Oklahoma. And the following year

26

at the Olympic Games, Jim Thorpe became known all over the world.

The Olympic Games are international sporting contests. They are held every four years. Athletes from many nations gather to compete in them. In 1912 they took place in Sweden.

Jim Thorpe represented the United States in the most difficult event of the Olympics, the decathlon. In Greek, *deka* means ten, and *athlos* means contest. The decathlon is a series of ten contests to select the best all-around athlete at the Games.

Jim won first place in four of the events, third place in four, and fourth place in two of the contests. His final decathlon score was more than 700 points higher than that of his nearest rival, a boy from Sweden.

At the ceremonies after the Olympics the King

of Sweden placed the victory medals around Jim's neck. Jim was now the best amateur athlete in the world.

When he returned to America, he was given a hero's parade in New York City. He was honored by the President of the United States in Washington. And he was mobbed by his joyous classmates at Carlisle. Newspapers published stories about his life.

One day Jim was called into Pop Warner's office.

"The Olympic authorities have asked me to talk to you," said Pop.

"What about, Coach?"

"They've been reading the newspaper stories about you. Is it true that you played baseball one summer in North Carolina?"

"Yes," Jim said, proud of the twenty-three games he had won.

"And did you receive pay for playing?"
"Yes, I did."
"Then you were a professional player."
"But I only earned fifteen dollars a week," Jim

protested. "Professional players earn thousands of dollars."

"It doesn't matter how much or how little," the coach explained. "If you took money at all, you were a professional. The Olympic Games are for amateurs only. You will have to return your medals."

Jim was stunned.

He took his medals to Pop Warner and they were returned to the Olympic authorities. Then, because of his sense of shame, he tried to hide himself. But newspaper reporters considered him news. They found him and wrote more stories about him.

Jim was lucky that they did. For he began to realize, slowly, that he was not in disgrace at all. Everyone understood that he had not intended to do anything wrong. In the hearts of most Americans he was forgiven.

The people in Europe forgave him, too. The Swedish boy he had beaten in the decathlon turned down the medals when they were offered to him.

"I won't accept them," he said. "They belong to Jim Thorpe. He is the best."

Jim then became a true professional athlete. He played both football and baseball for many years and earned a great deal of money. After he died, a movie was made about his life.

The medals he won have been placed in a museum in Switzerland, where they can be seen to this day. Jim Thorpe will always be remembered, by those who love sports, as America's greatest athlete.

ABOUT THE AUTHOR

Perhaps because his mother lived as a girl near the old Sac and Fox Agency in Indian Territory, Thomas Fall has been interested in Jim Thorpe since he was a small boy growing up in Oklahoma. Mr. Fall began actively collecting information about the famous athlete many years ago. He has visited the home of the Olympic hero and read everything about him he could find.

Mr. Fall can trace Cherokee ancestry in his own family. He is the author of many books for young people. He now lives in Brooklyn, New York.

ABOUT THE ILLUSTRATOR

John Gretzer has spent much of his life in the Midwest. He was born in Council Bluffs, Iowa; attended the University of Omaha; and spent one year at the Kansas City Art Institute, studying under Thomas Hart Benton.

Mr. Gretzer has been active in the production of animated movies and in department store advertising. He was at one time art director for a publishing firm, and now undertakes free-lance assignments involving advertising and editorial art. He is the illustrator of several books for children.

Mr. Gretzer and his family live in Perkasie, Pennsylvania.